My Grandmother's Last Letter

My Grandmother's Last Letter

Wendy Dunmeyer

LITERARY PRESS
LAMAR UNIVERSITY

ISBN: 978-1-962148-04-7
LOC: 2024933870

Cover Photo: zeys

Lamar University Literary Press
Beaumont, TX

To the Lord for always being with me,
and to LJW for teaching me to put God first.

To JGM: "Thank you" isn't big enough.

Recent Poetry from Lamar University Literary Press

Lisa Adams, *Xuai*
Walter Bargen, *My Other Mother's Red Mercedes*
David Bowles, *Liminal*
Jerry Bradley, *Collapsing into Possibility*
Mark Busby, *Through Our Times*
Julie Chappell, *Mad Habits of a Life*
Stan Crawford, *Resisting Gravity*
Glover Davis, *My Cap of Darkness*
William Virgil Davis, *The Bones Poems*
Jeffrey DeLotto, *Voices Writ in Sand*
Chris Ellery, *Elder Tree*
Dede Fox, *On Wings of Silence*
Alan Gann, *That's Entertainment*
Larry Griffin, *Cedar Plums*
Michelle Hartman, *Irony and Irrelevance*
Michael Jennings, *Crossings: A Record of Travel*
Gretchen Johnson, *A Trip Through Downer, Minnesota*
Betsy Joseph, *Only So Many Autumns*
Ulf Kirchdorfer, *Chewing Green Leaves*
Jim McGarrah, *A Balancing Act*
J. Pittman McGehee, *Nod of Knowing*
Laurence Musgrove, *A Stranger's Heart*
Benjamin Myers, *The Famiy Book of Martyrs*
Janice Northerns, *Some Electric Hum*
Nathaneal O'Reilly, *Landmarks*
Carol Coffee Reposa, *Sailing West*
Jan Seale, *The Parkinson Poems*
Steven Schroeder, *the moon, not the finger, pointing*
Glen Sorestad, *Hazards of Eden*
Vincent Spina, *The Sumptuous Hills of Gulfport*
W.K. Stratton, *Betrayal Creek*
Wally Swist, *Invocation*
Ken Waldman, *Sports Page*
Loretta Diane Walker, *Ode to My Mother's Voice*
Dan Williams, *At the Gates*
Jonas Zdanys, *The Angled Road*

For information on these and other Lamar University Literary
Press books go to www.Lamar.edu/literarypress

Your way was through the sea,
  your path, through mighty waters;
  yet your footprints were unseen.

—Psalm 77:19, NRSVA

. . . Full desertness,
In souls as countries, lieth silent-bare
Under the blanching, vertical eye-glare
Of the absolute Heavens. . . .

—Elizabeth Barrett Browning
"Grief"

. . . A poet's impulse to write also often comes from a sense of loss—
a hollow place which echoes inside. Poetry, perhaps, is that constant
searching for wholeness, alignment, kin.
    Poetry is also a searching for lineage, an inevitable recognition
of the echoes which reverberate in our life and work. . . . The themes
and structures of our poems embody shapes of the past and create new
reverberations. . . .

—Diane Thiel
Echolocations: A Brief Poetics

Acknowledgements

I am grateful to the editors of the following journals for publishing some of the poems in this collection:

Cumberland River Review
The Gold Mine
Measure
Natural Bridge
The Oklahoma Review
Sugar Mule

CONTENTS

Past Echo, New Reverberation
Sewanee, Tennessee

Perhaps it is the rain that falls, more rain
than usual for June, cleansing the air
and rinsing the plateau in sparkling greens.

Perhaps it is the cicadas, who hum
the summer's evening chorus to the pulse
of pregnant raindrops splashing oak and pine.

Perhaps it is the sister poet's hands,
whose silver-turquoise touch spins passion flowers
from broomsedge grasses, Lady-ferns, and sandstones.

Perhaps it is my fledgling self, with wings
outstretched to catch the wind and coast the stream
of earthy woman poet wreathed within.

Or perhaps it is your spectral form afloat
the rain, the hum, the hands, the wind, alive
and whispering, *Come sing with me.*

I.

Australia

From
the Latin
terra australis incognita,
the "unknown southern land"
Aristotle and Ptolemy both believed
existed as a massive continent cradling
the Indian Ocean to counterweight lands known
northward, the round Earth needing equal landmass
to maintain its symmetry and thus
not wander some cosmic arctic
outback forever lost like
a bandicoot on
a burnt
ridge.

Another Girl

Paddington, Brisbane
12 October 1923

I see a tiny hand uncurl—
my mum says, *Esther, it's a girl!*—
      and though I thank the Lord,
      I know we can't afford
this child, the third in three short years. . . .
Another girl. My husband hears
      the baby's feeble cries
      and from the doorway tries
to catch my eye, but I refuse
to look at him, to see him lose
      the gentle smile he's worn
      for months. *A boy*, he'd sworn,
I know this one's a boy! and I'd
prayed that he was right, had cried
      for God to heal his pain,
      to help him breathe, regain
his appetite. His fevers come
more often now, and blood let from
      his forearms to reduce
      his high blood pressure, loose
the swelling in his legs and face
doesn't help. I'd begged God's grace—
      but it's Bright's Disease, no cure,
      the doctor said, not sure
if Jesse's kidneys will fail, if he
will die. . . . Another girl. That's three.
      Dear Lord, he wanted a son.
      Your will, not ours, be done.

Toowong Cemetery
16 June 1924

The baby squeals and clasps her hands
on top her head to catch the wind
that dances through her curls and twirls
her pink silk ribbon like a leaf.
My father frowns, his eyebrow raised,
and coughs, his look a clear directive:
Correct that child, and make her stop.
I don't. I stare into his eyes
until he breaks and looks away.
He'd done the same when I'd refused
to dress the girls in black and white,
had met his *It's a funeral,*
not tea with Queen Elizabeth
with a silent stare, too sick
of darkened rooms and bleached bedsheets
to care about propriety.

I dressed the girls in pink and put
silk ribbons in their hair. I know
that Faith and Jessie are too young
to realize that their daddy's dead,
will not remember standing here
beside this bare black casket or
the preacher's stoic monotone,
will not remember that I pinned
a purple iris on my coat
because it was the flower Jess
had given me on our first date,
will not remember how he laughed
or called them all his lollies, sweet
enough to eat, but Rita might—

and if, as they grow up, she tells
her sisters about this day, I pray
that she'll remember—not how we
couldn't afford a few red roses
for his grave or how I stood
so stiffly, face and shoulders draped

in lace I'd taken from my wedding
veil and dyed this charcoal black—
but I pray that she'll remember how
the wind tugged at their ribbons just
the way their daddy used to do.

Cento to War[1]

Naked and cold like souls on Judgment Day,
the headstones yield their names to the element
among the apple-trees all bloom and scent
and all the decisive things still left to say.

They chide the loitering winds for their delay;
here war is harmless like a monument,
naked and cold like souls on Judgment Day.
The headstones yield their names to the element;

the earth is covered thick with other clay—
so secretly, like wrongs hushed-up, they went,
and every death for something different.
Unwillingly the spirit fled away,
naked and cold like souls on Judgment Day.

Air-Raid Drill
Brisbane, 1942

Tonight, as Jessie checked the blackout blinds
throughout the house, she vowed that she'd be brave,
not let the darkness blind her thoughts or let
the sirens pummel her knees like clapsticks.

But when the sirens rip her from her sleep
and her mother shouts, *Run to the shelter!*
her feet will not obey. *Dear Jesus, please,*
she whispers, staring at a sky ignited

by the searchlights' rays. *Dear Jesus . . . please,*
she falters once again before her lips
refuse to shape the prayer. She shuts her eyes
against the sirens' shrieks, the blackened street,

and sighs when silence floods her frame. *So nice,*
she thinks, not feeling how her mum tugs at
her hands. *So nice,* she thinks and wishes she
could rest forever in this vacant place.

I will be with you always. Jessie hears
the man's soft voice and turns to see his face,
but no one stands behind her . . . all she sees
is empty street. She doesn't understand.

She trusts that voice, so confident, serene,
and wants to call, "Where are you?" but to whom?
I will be with you always, Jess. Now go,
and in her head a chorus frees her feet.

Taking her mother's hand, she starts to sing
Onward, Christian Soldiers as she runs
toward the shelter through the sirens' screams.

Good-Time Girls

Before the war, we went to school. We learned
to cook and knit and keep a Christian home.
We dated boys our parents knew from church.
When Prince Albert, Duke of York, and his new wife,
the Lady Elizabeth, came to town,
we wore our Sunday dresses, stood along
the streets, and waved our nation's flag to show
the world our elegance. Back then, we were
Australia's virtues wrapped in calico,
good Aussie girls who'd make fine wives and rear
another generation like ourselves,

so good that when the war came, we were told
our patriotic duties were to serve.
Enlist or volunteer! our country urged,
while proud and smiling posters begged us join
the WAAAF or Women's Land Army though we
were trained to do so little, ornaments
meant to adorn some young man's arm and home.
But we did what we'd been taught to do: Obey.

We learned to sew and pack silk parachutes
and service planes. We learned to butcher pigs,
shear sheep, and harvest wheat. We learned to nurse
the wounded soldiers and wrote their letters home.
We welcomed all the Yanks at Red Cross dances
and served their tables at canteens. We did
what we were told, good Aussie girls, but when

these boys were charmed by us and we by them,
our parents, neighbors, priests, and government
called us Good-Time Girls and said we used
glamour and guile to trap the Yanks in marriage
and leave our homes behind to start new lives
as wealthy women in America.

Operation War Bride: Leaving Brisbane

"I am not one to discourage the realisation of love's young dream."
—Australian Prime Minister Ben Chifley, 8 March 1946

SS Mariposa
11 April 1946
6:25 a.m.
She feels the waves push miles between
her and the peaks and gullies steeped
in golden greens, the shrinking shades
of coastline, of her home, and blames
the briny sting of the Pacific
for her tears. Her hands clutch the ship's
steel rail, the rail that once embraced
Yank soldiers sailing on their way
to other islands, other fields.
She tries to shrug off the sun's heat,
too bright for her to wear, too foreign
for this Australian autumn morning.
If the sun would slide behind
a cloud, eclipse its dazzling light
and sparkling dance on top the sea,
then she could watch the coast recede
as it is buried by the sweep
of the horizon and the unknown
country she will now call home.

promises float

single pearls
    on starlit water

        lustrous round
            iridescence

        beckoning trust
but cultivated

silver lipped
    silver tongued

        cultured words
            glazing dips

        sways and swells
until swept to sea

by black lies
    breaking waves

Australian Makes Her Home Here
Based on an article in the Onawa Weekly Democrat

A happy reunion took place in Onawa
a couple weeks ago when the Australian wife
of Eric West, a local, lifelong resident,
arrived here in America.

The bride, the former Jessie Roberts of Brisbane,
and Mr. West married at the bride's family church
in that Queensland city. Mr. West met his wife
while he was stationed in Brisbane.

Mr. West served in the Pacific theatre
during the war. He spent three years in Australia,
New Guinea, and Manila, Philippine Islands,
until honorably discharged.

Once released from the Army Air Corps, Mr. West
arranged for his wife and her nine-months-old daughter
to join him at his home, a farm in Onawa.
They arrived here two weeks ago.

Mrs. West, a dental technician in Brisbane,
is well impressed with her home in America,
and while some things seem queer to her, she says she knows
she'll soon get used to all our ways.

Mr. West is a good man of fine character,
and *The Democrat* wishes for this young couple
a long, contented married life.

First Winter in America
Onawa, Iowa
November 1946

The snow lies two feet deep and still it falls.
Staring out the window, Jess recalls
the way her mother stood on the pier,
one hand clenched at her side, the other near
her chest. She watches as her daughter crawls

across the faded hardwood floor. Wool shawls
she'd brought from Brisbane can't ward off the squall's
cutting sullenness or her husband's sneer,
which, like the cold, lies deep. The snow still falls;

funny how, so white and light, it stalls
the days like brown-outs during the war. These walls,
unlike her mother's parlor, cannot cheer
her in her loneliness, too cold, severe
to feel like home. She shivers beneath her shawls.
The snow lies three feet deep and still it falls.

Virelai

Maybe it was helpless. I wanted it all,

the white farmhouse, the mountain's silhouette,
the porch swing swaying in an April sunset,
your quiet kiss, the lilac's scent at nightfall . . .

maybe it was helpless. I wanted it all,

but so did you, your pewter eyes as yet
unsettled, wandering, unwilling to forget
the smoke and waltz of other perfumed drawls.

Maybe it was helpless. Still, I wanted it all

with you, our home, our life, our unique duet
to the porch swing's rhythm in a spring sunset,
our minds and spirits melding each night's fall—

Maybe it was helpless. But I wanted it all.

To the Finder of This Letter—

I've been that literal wife, dinner
for two on the table, candles lit,
silverware and face aglow for a man
who never comes, never calls.

I've been her kind after a night
crying alone, shattered, voiceless
pain and prayers ricocheting off
heaven's floor and sinking, lost

in the abyss of the unanswered.

I've been burned by love imploding,
leaving ashes in its wake that swirl
this current eternity, too fine to be
netted, caught, and contained.

I've named my boat *Wings of the Wind,*
and with loneliness the only passenger
I now know and trust, I set sail,
toss my bottled tears into the sea,

and begin my wandering.

Old English Cento[2]

May I for my own self song's truth reckon
the Measurer's might and his mind plans
and the clear songs of skilled poets
meant to be a wonder of the world forever.

I am a lonely being, scarred by swords
present and past, but never more than now,
pacing the length of the patterned floor
on out into the ocean's sway. . . .

Over the sea, each dawn have I had care.
The news was known over the whole world—
nothing but war when I set off to join
the man who had lately landed among them.

He was well regarded, eager of mood,
and my heart longed to yield to him,
to take up my abode in a distant land
hung with hard ice-flakes, where hail-scur flew.

A ring-whorled prow rode in the harbor
on flood-ways to be far departing.
There I heard naught save the harsh sea.
No trembling harp. No tuned timber.

On the outlying coasts beyond the whale-road,
the land's expanses and the sky above.
My dress is silent when I tread the ground
among these people, my husband's kinsmen.

For twelve winters, seasons of woe,
my feet were by frost benumbed.
A fitting man, but one ill-starred, distressed,
friends and kinsmen flocked to his ranks.

I ever suffered grief, unleashed among in-laws
insensible to pain. He was overwhelmed.
His rage boiled over. So his mind turned.
Our marriage and our love had never been.

Dear lovers in this world lie in their beds;
bosque taketh blossom, cometh beauty of berries.
All I do is yearn. My own people,
they went down to death. I am left with nobody.

Head of the Heavens and High King of the World
more powerful than any man can know,
raise me above the dwelling place of men;
contrive to set at rest my careworn heart;

and clearly sing, when I am not in touch
with earth or water but a flying spirit,
for him who yearning longs for his beloved.

At-Home Delivery
21 June 1961
4:49 a.m.

The sun breaks orange-white across the sky
and drags the summer solstice to its start.
Two days ago, before my morning chores,
I'd read that in the *Farmers' Almanac,*
had read this day would last for fifteen hours
and fourteen minutes. *Thank You, Lord. More time,*
I'd thought. *More time to finish all the things*
I've left to do before this baby comes.
A fool. I've always been one, singing hymns
and praying to get through each day.

> I hear the truck door slam, the engine groan
> before it stutters to life, the crunch of tires
> on gravel as he heads toward the fields.
> Swallowing a bitter taste that floods
> my mouth, I lift the blankets off my legs
> and stand hunch-backed a moment till my limbs
> are strong enough to carry me across
> the floor and to my hours-old son.

I stare down at the ruddy face that's framed
with my dark hair, this change-of-life stranger
whose birth has made my husband smile with pride
for the first time in, well, I don't know how long.
I should pick up the baby, try to soothe
his muted cries, but I can't make my hands
reach out to lift him to my breast.

> I turn away. Through the bedroom door
> I see the dishes from last night piled high
> around the kitchen sink, the pots and pans
> unrinsed and slickened with uneaten greens
> and pork-chop fat. I see the dirty clothes
> I'd meant to wash before my labor pains
> got bad. The hens, I know, are pecking in
> the yard, impatient for their feed, their eggs
> in need of gathering, the overripe

31

tomatoes needing stewed and strained and canned
before they rot from all this heat. . . .

Slumping onto the floor beside the crib,
I prop my head between its spindled bars.
I wonder if we have a top-round roast
left in the freezer, wonder if, by chance,
my mother-in-law will drive the twenty miles
to see her newest grandchild and to bring
my daughters home.

                Why did he take them there?
    Both girls are old enough to have helped me through
    the birth. They knew about how scared I was
    to have a baby at my age, and they
    were worried, too, when he said no, I'd have
    this one out here, so far from town—

The girls would have believed me when I said
the baby wasn't going to come unless
I got some help, not told me to buck up,
that other wives delivered babies in
their beds at home without this fuss. . . .

    He told the doctor that we didn't have
    the money or the time to waste on needless
    hospital stays, insisted I come home.
    And when I hemorrhaged, blood gushing down
    my legs and pooling thickly at my feet,
    he handed me a towel and left the room,
    a faint *I'm sorry* all that he would say. . . .

I blink back the baby's mewl for milk,
pull my knees up to my chest, and wrap
my arms around myself, too tired to think
or face this fifteen-hour day.

Transformation
After Diane Thiel's "Continuum"

Is it about selfless love or lack of self-worth?
Is there some line we cross when we are finally worthless,
when we see straight into our abuser's mind
and find some logic in the fibers knit?

Where is that line—was it one muggy Wednesday morning,
the way the heat unraveled that remaining strand of self?
The making of excuses brings you closer
every time. It might look like so much weakness

spindled through a life—whirled, dropped, then twisted
to know the way the pain was crucial in that reshaping
of the thread—first to forgive—and then slowly to accept
the blame, believe it's all your fault. Though you always carry

the old you like a tear, you find the way to hide the hole,
and in the making of excuses, you know you are alone.

Another Washing-Day

She marks the mindless passing of each day
by counting loads of laundry she has done:
a good, productive day, say five or six;
a bad day, one or two. It never ends,
this sort-then-wash-and-dry-and-fold routine
the rut in which she spins. The last load in,

she sighs and turns to start another chore.
Before she takes a step, her teen-aged son
appears and dumps a pile of t-shirts, jeans,
and socks into an empty basket—proof
of life beyond this house he's harvested
from his bedroom floor. She looks away,
her lips pressed closed. But when the washer starts
its shaky spin and walks across the worn
linoleum she'd picked out in the pitch
of early homeowner bliss, she snaps, her mind
unable to accept the washer's nerve,
its free-will freedom to travel where it wants
though plugged into a semi-glossed white wall.

She slams up the lid to stop the washer, rams
her hip against its side, and back it slides,
an inch, then two, then three, until it sits
straight in its place. A curved indention marks
the washer's front, a purple bruise her hip,
and when her husband later asks about
the dent, she shrugs and presses her fingertips
into her hidden bruise.

Vegemite

It looked like axle grease.
That's how we grandkids described it,
out of your hearing, of course,
after we'd stood by the toaster
one frigid winter morning and watched
you slather two perfectly lovely pieces
of white-bread toast. We didn't think
you'd eat it. We couldn't imagine
you cutting each slice, putting one corner
in your mouth, taking a bite, and
chewing that goo with such delicate
enjoyment. We couldn't imagine you
doing this but watched as you did,
horror and disgust sliding across
our faces. You couldn't convince us
to try a bite. We knew you were crazy—
we'd seen how Grandpa silenced you
with one low *No*, how you'd knot
your fingers, push your hands
into your lap, a stuttered *Th-that-tuh*
stumbling off your tongue as your eyes
fell to the floor. We'd heard
our mothers say, *She's so far out there,
completely nuts*, as they rolled their eyes—
We weren't. We watched. We knew.
So we refused to sample even the smallest
taste of your childhood, afraid
we'd wind up crazy like you.

All Along: The Quiet One Keeps the Sabbath

In her gray and pink
Sunday dress, she pads
past clutches of small talk
and tight smiles,

the talcum-scented
butterflies flitting from
rumor to rumor

and the starched, stoic
lions hidden amid
the gossip, lying wait
to pounce or purr as called.

She whispers past, head down,
eyes bowed, wordless pain
inspiring her way,

still seeking her God,
His grace, His salvation.
Once outside, she lifts
her head in unspoken

prayer, her upturned eyes
meek and pure in heart
as cloudless heaven,

and searching, finds Him there.

Daughter of God[3]
Beto shel Elohim

Impress these words of Mine on your heart:
How beautiful you are, My darling!

As beautiful as the full moon, as pure as the sun,
I have inscribed you on the palms of My hands;
I have called you by name; you are Mine!
You are like the wings of a dove covered with silver.

Impress these words of Mine on your soul:
My darling, how beautiful you are!

I have loved you with an everlasting love.
Trust in the Lord with all your heart,
Trust in the Lord and do good,
And I will give you rest.

Impress these words of Mine on your heart and on your soul:
How beautiful you are, My darling, how beautiful you are!

Heaven
After Billy Collins' "The Future"

When I finally arrive there—
and I hope it will not be much longer—
I like to believe God will be waiting
and might even tell me I did well.

So He will remind me of a Bible lesson I taught
or a child for whom I made a rag doll
or the time I knit an iris-purple tam
for a woman who'd lost her hair to chemotherapy.

Then He will open on a pedestal
the heavy book in which my life is written
and explain to me where I went wrong
but that He loves me, anyway—

despite how I disobeyed my mother
when she told me not to marry him,
despite how I lied again and again
when things weren't fine or good,

despite how I believed my husband's lies
each time he called me weak and worthless
and faithless and made me feel so small
when I simply should have left him—

and God will listen, mild-eyed and forgiving,
while I cry the last of my human pain,
like a ship moving toward,
not away from, the coastline it calls home.

Poem

The wooden garden angel hangs
looped on a shepherd's hook, her knees
and shoulders knots of rusted wire,
the same stained wire that shapes her small,
round wings,

her sun-bleached robe accessorized
with two hand-painted violets, pink
and blue, their anthers the other's hue,
a faded-angel metaphor
for grace,

the mercy placed by God in nature,
even a one-by-four-foot plot
that nurtures iris bulbs beneath
a pock-marked concrete porch just large
and loved

enough to hold a rocking chair
and tiny table petrified
by thirty summers' suns and winds
and constant dish-cloth dusting of
the frail,

white-haired, house-dressed woman who,
once seeking her salvation, saw
a need to hang the angel there.

Elderly Woman Rocking

In her walnut rocking chair she watches
twilight ripen into dawn her backward
forward swaying a glissade into the
dim blue hours past silhouettes sighing
whispering as they pirouette through swirling
twirling leaves the skitter skirring of her
memories a grande jete the leaping
gliding guides her back in time between their
gray illuminations and the morning
light she watches from her rocking chair

Solo Flight

A single-engine airplane hums
above the clouds somewhere unseen.
While she sits and works her sums,
a single-engine airplane hums.
Brushing away eraser crumbs,
she gazes through the window screen;
a single-engine airplane hums
above the clouds somewhere unseen.

A single-engine airplane soars
in cursive script across the sky.
While she tends her housewife chores,
a single-engine airplane soars.
Brushing away dreams unexplored,
she smiles to hide a lonesome sigh;
a single-engine airplane soars
in cursive script across the sky.

A single-engine airplane lands
on a runway in a field.
While she wrings her age-stained hands,
a single-engine airplane lands.
Brushing away death's sharp demands,
she won't allow her dreams to yield;
a single-engine airplane lands
on a runway in a field.

this is it

this is some of my life
hope you get something out of this
hope you have wonderful lives

remember me
remember to live for God
remember to keep God first
He will help you have wonderful lives

God bless you
God keep you
God was kind to me
God blessed and kept us together

this is it

Roots Music

The starlit mountains echo promises,
uncluttered lullabies, the sighs of leaves.
Coyotes chorus call responses
as starlit mountains echo promises
and firs lift wordless prayers like prophecies.
The wind amid the rustic roses grieves
while starlit mountains echo promises,
uncluttered lullabies, the sighs of leaves.

II

Importance of Words

I first learned the importance,
        the weight and power and permanence,
of words

when I was three years old. Alone,
        breath razed, I cried and begged
my father

to stop beating me with his belt,
        Black and long and two inches thick,
he bragged

while he whipped me with intent
        to bruise and break and violate.
He refused.

He refused, used his arm to pin me,
        thin and unclothed, against his knees,
his belt

uncoiling, striking as he hissed,
        Shut up. Stop crying. Tell anyone,
and you'll

have hell to pay.

Momma Doesn't Love Me

That's what she says, and
what she means is
she doesn't want me.
She wishes I
were never born.

That's what she says and
what she means when
she breaks the yardstick
across my back,
bruises the belt

across my thighs—
that's how I learn
to spell my name
and tie my shoes.
Stupid girl.

That's what she says, and
what she means is
if she, my momma,
doesn't want me,
doesn't love me—

That's what she says, and
what I believe
is true—if Momma
doesn't want me,
doesn't love me—

Why would you?

Reverberations

I line the edges of my bed
with Lincoln Logs, my slinky dog,
my Etch-A-Sketch, and all the toys
I think will fall with lots of noise
onto the hardwood floor, then lie
beneath my blankets with my arms
clutched tightly around my Giggles doll
and pray the Lord my soul to keep.

I need to stay awake. I stare
out of my window at the sky
and with my finger trace around
the shadow of the old pine tree
that grows in our front yard. I draw
connect-the-dot star pictures, find
the brightest star and make a wish—
I try to stay awake but can't.

From somewhere in my dreams, a voice
whispers my name. I blink awake
and look toward my bedroom door,
a black and empty hole. I hold
my breath and pray, *Dear Jesus, please,*
I ask that You will keep me safe
and help me to be brave, but when
my father stalks into my room,

I scramble off my bed and crawl
confused across the toy-strewn floor.
I try but cannot find the door.
He grabs me, drags me to the bed,
my throat contracting soundless screams
that ever after echo through my core.

Bedtime Prayers

Each day our momma cleaned with equal parts
of water and ammonia, mixed that strong,
she said, because the good Lord only knew
what filthy things we'd smeared, disgusting pigs,
throughout her house. We tried to hide our red,
cracked hands behind our backs, afraid she'd find

imagined dirt beneath our nails and beat
us with the leather belt that bruised our hips
and thighs before she'd make us soak our hands
in that burning mixture. We'd learn, she said,
that if we'd just obey our mother, then
we wouldn't have to pray each night, *Dear God,*
We're sorry that we made our momma yell.
Please forgive our sins and don't send us to hell.

From Childhood into Adulthood

My momma whips a black trash bag
against the wall and screams, *You're stupid,*
worthless, both of you! Again
the bag explodes against the wall.
A jar inside shatters and cracks
the sheetrock in a moon-shaped arc.
Stray shards of glass, wet coffee grounds,
and sour Frosted Flakes splatter on
the floor. *I hate this house, this life. . . .*

I say, *Um, Momma?* but my throat
chokes back the words. I swallow, try
again. *Hey, Momma? I need your help.*
I wish that I had phrased that better,
pray that Momma hasn't heard,
but Momma spins around and yells,
You're asking me for help?, then swings
her fist.

      The punch lands on my cheek.
I beg, *Please, Momma, stop*, and turn
to run but fall. From down the hall,
my sister cries, a muted *Oh!*
and stumbled breaths.

           I look into
my momma's eyes. *I need your help.*
I got my period. I don't
know what to do. Dropping her fist,
my momma nods and walks into
the bathroom.

        Silently, I do
what I am told, then go into
my bedroom, curl up on my bed,
and cry until my cheek and chest
are numbed.

Up Grandma's cobbled footpath

stones reaped from corn fields
and replanted in the slope

past her roses swaying
beside the back-porch steps

past her irises nodding
along the back-porch rails

past her farmhouse garden
rhubarb lush in the corner
tomatoes tripping off vines

up to the maple tree's arms
wide and deep and shading

the John-Deere tire swing
swaying on grey rope

the cradle in which I nestle
frail as a newly-hatched wren
to bind my child wounds

Worldlines

In a backroad, backyard world,
       people look skyward.
Clapboard houses and corn fields
       shape desires and dreams,

       sun-burnt and wind-blown
in daylight's yellow-dirt, split-rail reality,
       moon-cooled and renewed
in nighttime's sweeping, tire-swing vision,

external facts
       earthly, short-lived,
internal fictions
       heavenly, endless.

Wallflower

She sits alone and silent in a swirl
of pulsing adolescent disruption,
her blonde hair pulled into a ponytail
except for one bold curl that spirals down
her back out of control. Her blue eyes, soft
and make-up free, survey the floor then girls
whose smooth, straight hair and smoky-shadowed eyes
inspire the boys to horseplay, broken-voiced
attempts at conversation, or displays
of simple gallantry, like holding doors.
Her slender fingers tremble in her lap,
and if she were aware of that, she'd sit
on them to silence their timidity.
Her feet, however, clad in pink-and-green-
plaid tennis shoes, tap out a beat, a pulse
of inner self-sufficiency, a hint
that though she's not yet found her niche, she will.

Cover Story[4]
for my mother

You act compliant,
        soft, flexible,
your cover smooth,
        clean, creaseless,

but you are laminate,
        clear veneer
with thin-ply cardboard
        underneath,

a snapshot still-life
        Greek amphora,
burnt-orange glaze
        and black-figure

silhouette broken,
        eroded by
burial and time,
        an excavated

shadow preserved
        as art or
living history
        but no longer

utile in the real,
        tangible world.

Old Spice and Listerine

And I think we also now know that the same part of the brain that
governs smell is engaged in higher thought, and it's where everything
comes from; everything kind of comes out of a sense of smell. . . .
—A.E. Stallings

Forced to forgive you to save
my self, I have survived. But

my body refuses to forget,
its physical senses driven by

my primordial pain, pain seared
into my body's memories,

denying my mind release.

This is why, a lifetime later,
I walk through Walmart, maybe,

or wander the poetry section
at the public library, minding

my own, lost in my own, and
the smell of Old Spice freezes

me, hand mid-air to lift fresh
bread or Stallings' *Olives*

from a shelf, spirals me back
to childhood, to your naked

white form filling the frame
of my bedroom doorway,

to your crushing me, breaking
my body beneath the flowered

blanket on my full-sized bed.

This is why, a lifetime later,
though now supposedly I'm safe,

the smell of Listerine expels
my grasp on everything, propels

my feet out the nearest exit,
blinds my eyes terror-wide,

eradicates my pulse with fear.

The White Coyote

The cattle rancher doesn't think twice.
He sees her fur lift in the southerly wind
that brushes the bluestem prairie grass,
aims his rifle, fires, and watches her hips

swing out and collapse. He doesn't wait
for her to die. Grabbing a rusted coil
of barbed wire discarded by the barn,
he runs across the field. She watches him come,

then drops her head on her front paws,
her eyes tamed by pain, her quavering howl
silenced by labored breath. Her latest kill,
a slender cottontail to feed her pups,

lies at her side. The rancher stops short;
he hadn't seen the rabbit in her mouth,
hadn't known she wasn't stalking his herd.
The grass goes still with her last breaths.

He strokes her head, clenches his shaking hand.
Too late to change what he has done,
he seizes her by the scruff, wraps the wire
three times around her neck, and hangs her

from a pine fence post, her rare white fur
a warning to other predators.

On Seeing the Hunt at Dusk

The table cleared, the dishes washed, the kids
both bathed and tucked in bed, I go outside
to sit on the front porch and watch the moon
rise orange over a horizon framed
by thin green clouds.

                Beyond the split-rail fence,
cicadas sing tympanic choruses,
while on the rain-damp lawn a mother skunk
and her two kits forage for roots and bees.
The momma pauses, cocks her head to scratch
behind her ear. The kits, intent on play,
come tumble over her. She shakes them off
and walks away, her kits in close pursuit,
her lot and mine so similar, I sigh.

A small brown doe steps from behind a hedge
of rusty blackhaw shrubs. With white tail tucked,
she bends her head to browse as lightning bugs
glitter among the leaves.

                In fluid grace,
a cougar leaps onto her back, embeds
his claws in her front flanks. The doe rears back;
the cougar clamps her throat between his teeth,
and with a twist, he breaks her neck. She blinks,
then crumples to the ground in silent folds.

I run into the house and take the steps
two at a time up to the nursery,
where in the nightlight's glow my children sleep.
I hear their steady breaths but cannot calm
my own. I turn away.

                The curtains lift
and fall. I stand between their sway and watch
the cougar drag his kill toward the dark.

PTA Mothers

After flittering on their social lives, they light upon the embarrass-
ment of mothers who must pry from their thighs the fingers of
their offspring on that first day of kindergarten.

The brunette taps French-manicured fingertips on her khak-
ied knee and states she refused to be one of those mothers. She
trained her children. Once a week, she took them to Mommy's Day
Out so they would not embarrass her on their first days of school.

The redhead dangles a Gucci sandal from her coral toes and states
she avoided a first-day scene by promising her children ice-cream
cones if they did not cry and cling.

The PTA mothers laugh, etiquette laughter expiring in sighs.

I imagine their faces were I to confess how, no training or bribery
needed, my daughter said, *Love you, Momma*, tugged her hand
from mine, skipped off with a wave, and left me standing outside
her classroom doorway on her first day of school.

I imagine their faces were I to confess how, as my daughter
skipped into kindergarten, I walked home, suddenly alone and
crying.

storm

how mild
the sudden calm,
as soft as infant's breath,
before the wind-whipped clouds coalesce
and roar

Deployment Formation

Fort Sill, Oklahoma
19 February 2003
0430 Hours

You stand beneath the floodlight's glare, feet set,
hands clasped behind your back, parade-rest stance,
while I, behind the rope line, stand intent
and praying that you'll turn for one last glance
that never comes. The soldiers to your right
and to your left are now your sole concern,
the battle buddies with whom you'll go fight.
The colonel's voice commands, *We all return—*
we all come home. My fingers clutch my throat,
catch on your old dog tags, each ball-chain bead
a small but binding promissory note
on which I'll count each day till you're with me.
      Beneath your unit's artillery guidon,
      you march away into the dark predawn.

At 3 A.M.

I

20 March 2003

At 3 a.m. she lies in bed and stares
at the Iraqi skyline on TV.
She waits—for what? His unit? Humvee? Face?

A thunderstorm erupts. Lightning cracks
the darkness, snaps two branches of an elm,
and sends them toppling down the roof's incline.

Her bedroom window shatters when they fall.

II

1 July 2003

His colonel pins the Bronze Star to his chest,
shakes his hand, and praises his bravery.
He doesn't meet the colonel's eyes or hers.

*A bodiless hand still grips the Jeep's roll bar,
the fingers thick, the nails eclipsed with dirt,
the palm rough—an Iraqi soldier's hand.*

It looks just like his dad's. A farmer's hand.

III

4 July 2003

His weekend uniform: pajama pants,
a Harley tee, and slippers. Nightmares blitz
his sleep. He doesn't shower, shave, or speak.

Two boys squat in the middle of the street,
unwrap a package, light its fuse, and run.
The M-80 echoes like rocket fire.

Taking cover, he pulls his wife to the floor.

IV

4 April 2003

Three M16s stand, their bayonets thrust
into the sand with boots on either side
and Kevlar helmets resting on their stocks.

Three sets of dog tags hang and sway and clank
from the weapons' pistol grips. The wind
accuses him: You trained him. Now he's dead.

The soldier he ate breakfast with is dead.

V

11 September 2003

She eyes the cold, uneaten pot roast, checks
the time again, and wonders where he is.
With shaking hands, she starts to call his friends.

He hands a longneck to the blonde and drinks
another six before he takes her home.
He doesn't know her name and doesn't care.

He slaps his wife when she asks where he's been.

VI

4 April 2003

Opening fire, Iraqi soldiers hit
a Humvee, watch it burn. They disappear
in bunkers underground. Blood clots the sand.

The CO calls off each dead soldier's name,
followed by KIA. A moment's silence;
the unit bows their heads; the chaplain prays.

He wakes up screaming, *No more, God. No more.*

VII

20 March 2004

In a motel miles away from home,
she cries in bed, watches *Headline News,*
and listens as hailstones pelt the windows.

At home, he's passed out in the truck's front seat,
his forehead on the steering wheel, his dog tags
dangling from the rearview mirror.

His unit mounts and rolls toward Baghdad.

After a Summer Drought

Raindrops tumble from blades of grass and bounce when they hit the soil. Bluestem grasses, hickories, hydrangeas, clovers and violets and black-eyed Susans—none have been this green, this white, this red and lavender and yellow since April, when spring rains stopped and the sun slowly scorched the horizon and its reaches taupe. Brown-gray leaves spun on brown-gray branches, then let go, spiraled across blanched grasses and scuttled against fence lines. Corn stalks dried ramrod straight, row upon row like soldiers in desert camouflage, curled shucks at parade rest. In this aridity, only cotton flowered, unfolded pink blooms that faded to perfect white boles. Cottontail rabbits browsed farther and farther from their burrows, risking daylight beneath hawks' hungry red eyes. Bats stopped hunting bugs above the trees and instead swooped porchlights to forage their evening meals. Even the ancient barn owl left his oak-tree nest to sit on a barbed-wire fence and scout for mice. One brief July rain served only to make everything thirst more.

But now, the air is fragrant with wildflowers and pine needles. Now, the paths we walk are pillowed with wet leaves and moss. Now, the prairies ready their native colors for harvest. Now, we bathe in mist and scent and quiet and color and, in doing so, find ourselves again.

A Mild December

                    Squirrels, fat in fall,
are thin, their haunches honed to bone, their tails
spiked and pale amid the broomsedge grass
they forage, seeking acorns still; the warm,
dry wind and ground forestall creation's call
for them to rest and feed from stores they've dug
beneath the leafless post oaks. Killdeer peck
the roadside rocks for beetles, errant seeds
prevented purchase in the furrowed fields,
while rabbits quiver to catch scents of clover
that never come. All nature waits, inured
by instinct, sure of winter's claim, yet held
bewildered by the sun's hypnotic sway.

fatigue

ashes tumble
from the Marlboro
suspended
between his lips
as he quick-times
up one block,
down another,
the only PT
his retired,
arthritic feet,
hands, and neck
can execute

his feet
pound concrete,
but his mind,
clouded by
shield and storm,
marches sand
that when he wakes
at 2, 3, 4 a.m.
still grits his
teeth and tongue

Strange Reflection

Beneath her bathroom's bright white light, she peers
into the mirror as she styles her hair,
a task she thinks is pointless. All those years
she wasted trying to look good, the care,

the effort she painstakingly believed
would keep her young: the toners, facials, soaps,
and moisturizers she once used deceived
her naïve vanity with their false hopes

and thirty-day, money-back guarantees—
as if, at twenty-five years old, four weeks
of soft, clear skin meant she had found the means
to stop the lines now worn across her cheeks.

What does it matter if she showers, dresses,
does her hair, or puts on makeup? All
she does these days is clean up the messes
her children and her husband make and haul

the kids to school, the mall, and anywhere
else they want to go. She doesn't need
a manicure, a pedicure, a pair
of Bruno Magli platform heels to feed

her family dinner or to wash five loads
of laundry every day. Her fingers try
to hide a strand of errant gray that goads
her patience by refusing to comply.

She sighs and wants to turn away before
she makes eye contact with the mask she knows
lurks inside the glass, but she cannot ignore
this strange reflection with the eyes and nose

and lips and chin she doesn't recognize—
She sees each facial feature's shape distinct
against her fading skin, but each defies
her memory as if she were extinct.

Terpsichore

As constant as the Oklahoma wind
that whips the dust into a devil's dance,
she waits for him while twilight fades to dark.

She's played his waiting game before. The dark
in gentle whisper beckons on the wind
a serenade to which she wants to dance,

just like she did when as a child she'd dance
and twirl until all colors, light and dark,
whirled like leaves tossed by an autumn wind—

windswept, she dances duet with the dark.

Reminiscence

Your voice dives,
cliff-like,
down an octave,

and I know
your next
words will hurt, dull

needles thrust
through my
midnight-blue skin.

Overhead, hawks
whir wind,
chasing clouds

as the sun fades
gray-gold
the broomsedge

grasses where, as
children,
we ran, hid,

whispered, held
hands, and
one dusk shared our

first kiss, close-
lipped, chaste
but lingering

until your
sister's
sing-song *Olly*

*olly oxen
free!* sent
us running

home to grandmas,
porch swings,
and fireflies,

constellations
we caught
and contained. . . .

Mason-jar memories
neglected, abandoned,

dreams lost like pennies
in high prairie grasses.

I still love you

your note to me this morning reads,
and I want to tear it up,

cram each piece down your throat until,
raw and bruised, your throat burns like

mine burned last night as I swallowed
words with which you stoned me, but

I don't.

Instead, I trim your note to size,
tape it between two blank, blue

pages in my journal, and flip
back and forth around it as

I write, ignoring it until
prayer and pages blunt my own

fist full of stones.

No Sale

I wear the label "your wife"
like high-water jeans—
two inches too short
and with the holes
in my Keds exposed
for public ridicule.

*Men always scope out
what's out there,* you say,
a one-size-fits-all excuse
for your lack of moral fiber.

But just as I'm not
the one-night stand
to whom you offer
your Wranglers and
your bed, I'm also not
the cut-rate woman
willing to settle for
your clearance-rack love.

III

Backwoods, Tennessee

Sunlight fills spaces
between weather-warped
boards of barn after
barn built when farmsteads
formed America's
frontier,

      whitewashes
fences framing rows
of wooden crosses
carved with family names,
pioneer pride, home-
spun independence,

and sweeps porches to
cabins still standing,
however tattered
or tottering, in
spring's greens and blues, hues
and history held

captive, secluded
in these bootleg hills.

Miles and Smoke

Highways turned back roads disappear between
hickories, pines, and sandstone cliffs that scrape
the Cumberland Plateau. These wooded bluffs
don't speak, concealing pain in family plots
and moonshine lethal as living feuds. Here, regret
is sharp, and grief is silent. Widow's tears
and ridges know where bodies lie, where lies
hide truth and truth erodes in loneliness.
        Driven from home, I sought the solace of
these slopes, their caves and ravines tombs in which
my voiceless grief could rest. But here, where vultures
brood in wait for carcasses to devour,
I find a thousand miles and smoke-mute hills
are not enough to silence your apathy.

moonrise

behind a blue moon's
        mountain silhouette,
black ridges burst
        into white flame,

setting fire to fir, birch,
        scrub oak, and hickory,
melting magnolia and moonflowers,
        mystifying tentative deer

and sultry mountain lions,
        who lift bowed heads,
eyes unblinking, and listen
        as cicadas drop mid-chorus

their haunting midnight thrums

Fall Field Crickets

I

Crickets invade
     my aloneness

uninvited,
     their acoustic

radiations
     hidden discords

stridulating
     from dark closets,

darkest corners
     beneath the bed,

bookshelf, sofa,
     even between

stovetop burner
     coil and plate, where

one trills tease chirps
     confident in

undetection
     until sullen

September rains
     drive me to crave

potato soup,
     and the suspect

leaps out with a
     screech and scorched wings.

II

December snows;
        the crickets left

for wherever
        crickets winter.

Silence echoes
        their haunts, their call

court, and triumph
        songs echoic

memories, sounds
        white as windows

frost flecked, opaque,
        too cold to see

beyond.

North Winds

Redwood window box,
winter empty,

soil infertile, frost
and frozen winds

leaving in their wake
flaked erosion,

life breaths blown away
in dust puffs faint

as abandoned dreams.

The Privilege I Claim for My Own Sex
After Jane Austen's Persuasion

You need not covet it,
our loving longest when all hope is gone.
You've had every advantage, pens of wit—
so no, you need not covet it.
This is, perhaps, our fate and not our merit,
how we can't help ourselves though you've withdrawn.
No, you need not covet it,
our loving longest when all hope is gone.

Resolution

1 January, 11:52 AM

Because I can't go on waking up,

drinking two bottles of water,
then two cups of coffee with creamer,

reading a Bible chapter before
stumbling through failing-faith prayers,

both out loud because faith comes
from hearing, hearing from
the word of God, and I need faith,

both out loud because I need to hear
a human voice, even if only my own . . .

Because I can't go on hiding in

this one-bedroom apartment
alone and afraid of going outside

and seeing lovers, husbands,
wives, families, those connections

I loved hard for but lost, somehow,
watching for your text or
phone call that never comes,

wanting to stop loving you like you
did me—but how?—I don't know how . . .

Because I can't go on waiting for you—

I'm letting you go.

I Am . . .

a daughter of God,
>*Beto shel Elohim.*

I am created by God, for God—
>not a mistake,
>not crazy,
>not spiritually weak.

I am loved.

I am created by God, for God—
>planned for,
>wonderfully made,
>pure in heart.

I am blessed.

I am created by God, for God—
>in His image,
>for His purpose,
>on His right side.

I am never alone.

I am created by God, for God—
>shielded by Michael,
>covered in a mantle,
>protected and placed.

I am set apart.

I am created by God, for God—
>a seer,
>a visionary,
>a discerner.

I am gifted.

I am defined by God, and no one else.

I am a daughter of God,
>*Beto shel Elohim.*

tanka

a streetlamp's blue light

  translucent in falling snow

    echoes in his eyes

  the spirit's lonely refrains

she whispered and he answered

Acceptance

Relax, he says, a gentle guy with whom
she just agreed to go to dinner. *Please . . .*
you need to just relax. She smiles, she nods,
she knows he's right, but silently she curses
her fallen breasts, her slackened belly, burnt
remains she offered in self-sacrifice
to marriage, motherhood, and middle age,
remains her now ex-husband left behind
because he didn't want her anymore—

she sees her self, naked, scarred, alone—

and prays the longing that propels her to
this place beyond the labels "wife" and "mom"
will not humiliate the woman she
must now embrace as who she is.

Medium aevum

It sounds quite nice in Latin, nicer than it feels, this middle place between lost youth and *geras*—Greek; "old age"—but it's medieval.

Not just to you 20-somethings who don't yet believe that 50 is the new 30, but to us, too, we souls whose body parts were fine one night before we went to bed but razed by dawn with no Notice of Demolition served to warn us of their fleet departure south.

No, we don't want to see ourselves naked, either. In fact, we wonder why, after 50, full body lifts are not considered medical necessities.

And that *With-age-comes-wisdom* thing? Well, we'll get back to you on that as soon as we remember why we ever thought that everyone over 45 was old.

Yes, we once believed that, too. But standing on the other side of 50 changed our points of view.

We weren't ready for it, this middle place. Losing youth—the strength, the immortality we loved—we didn't intentionally lie to ourselves. It's evident now, however, that the art of aging is hard to master.

No, we weren't ready for it, this medieval middle age. And though we know it's coming—we know it's coming—it *is* coming—

We just aren't ready to be—*Say* it!—old.

The Common Lilac

Prune it too much, and it responds
with new growth but no flower.
Young branches need time
to develop, strengthen, and blossom.

Its mature, stout stems, however,
furrowed and flaking grey,
flower year after year,
dependable as spring.

Rocky slopes, dry soil, full sun,
cool climates, winter's frost—
it requires life's roughness
to thrive and produce at its peak;

yet, in its peasant hardiness,
it needs to stretch its branches
and unfurl its heart-shaped leaves
to frame its panicles,

which keep their bloom a week or two
before its fruits produce their two-winged seeds.

Calliope's Rules

I ain't gonna tell you, *Girl,*
you have to get in shape! Mercy me,
you're 53, and face it, baby,
there be some things just fall
into their own ways of bein'
no matter how hard you try
to force 'em to conform.

I ain't gonna tell you, *Child,*
don't you stamp your foot like that!
Doin' that would be like tryin' to stop
a two-year-old from sayin' "No!"
Ain't never gonna happen,
fact's a fact, and honey,
ain't nobody perfect all the time.

I ain't gonna tell you, *Miss,*
a lady minds her p's and q's!
It's a truth can't be denied, darlin',
that there are times a real lady
must come off her best behavior
to make herself be heard.

I ain't gonna tell you, *Ma'am,*
you'd best watch your mouth! Heavens,
I do that, then I gotta watch my own,
so'd everybody else on this planet,
and the whole dang world'd go mute.

Lines

> *. . . the line is the differentia of verse and prose: through
> out most of recorded history, poetry has been cast in
> verse, and verse set in lines. . . .*
> —The New Princeton Encyclopedia of Poetry and Poetics,
> "Line"

I am different. Been told I was a *tree hugger* for leaving my backyard unmowed
                                          one spring when wild
butterfly peas with lavender lines and daisy fleabane with white and yellow florets
                                          rayed a watercolor
palette across the red clay dressed in gray buffalograss, for leaving local flora spin
                                          recorded prose to verse.

I am different. Told I *dress like a writer*, whatever that means, as if cardigans,
                                          white socks, and white canvas
shoes worn with skirts, jeans, everything, and adapted to any occasion were
                                          some crazy sister-poets'
secret uniform, a cast by which we are identified but which non-poetic laity can't
                                          designate or define.

I am different. Told I'd *never use* my propensity for reading and writing poetry
                                          in the real world
and then scolded again for rejecting that world because their real isn't mine—
                                          but why would I
want in it if I can't be me? To be a mere metonymy? A synecdoche, a part of me
                                          but never whole?

I am different. Bathed in moonlight in winter nights, I taste snowflakes like words
                                          and wind like rhyme.
I hear iambs in eagle wings, caesuras in sunflowers, rondelets in rocks, hymns
                                          in buffalo horns.
I am different. I am me: Tree-hugging, writer-clad, unrealistic. A poet lineated,
                                          a verse set in lines.

On a Wing

Like an eagle glides, I might
      take flight in eccentricity,
           circle clouds, coast currents,

finish with a fancy free-
      fall dive, flirt with earth, death, decay,
           then wing the wind away,

an urchin opposed to
      order. To roll right on cue, to
           stick to the subject at hand—

I'm done for. I can't. I doubt
      I'll ever get the hang of that.

Clearing up the Question of the Drop Bear's Existence
After Anne Carson

1. Either the drop bear exists or he does not.

2. If he exists, either the drop bear is an Australian marsupial or he is not.

3. If he is an Australian marsupial, the drop bear resembles either a super large koala or a kangaroo.

4. If he resembles a super large koala, the drop bear either has canine teeth or does not have canine teeth and instead has strong premolars.

5. If he has canine teeth, either the drop bear uses them to eat bark and meat or he does not eat at all.

6. If he uses his canine teeth to eat bark and meat, either the drop bear inhabits gum trees or he does not.

7. If he inhabits gum trees, either the drop bear hunts by dropping from gum-tree branches onto his ground-walking prey or he does not.

8. If he hunts by dropping from gum-tree branches onto his ground-walking prey, either the drop bear attacks humans or he does not.

9. If he attacks humans, either the drop bear stuns them by biting their necks and dragging them back up the gum tree to feed without other carnivores bothering him or he does not.

10. If the drop bear stuns his human prey, bites their necks, and drags them back up the gum tree to feed, human beings can take precautions against drop bear attacks or not take any precautions at all.

11. If they take precautions against drop bear attacks, human beings either can put Vegemite or toothpaste behind their ears or can wear forks in their hair.

12. If they put Vegemite or toothpaste behind their ears, human beings might want to know that there is no evidence to support claims that these precautions work or they might not.

13. If they might want to know that there is no evidence to support claims that these precautions work, human beings also might want to know how to tell if a drop bear is hiding in a gum tree or they might not.

14. If they also might want to know how to tell if a drop bear is hiding in a gum tree, human beings either can lie on their backs beneath a gum tree and spit upwards or they can not.

15. If human beings lie on their backs beneath a gum tree and spit upwards, the drop bear will indicate that he is up that tree by spitting back or he will not.

16. If he spits back, either the drop bear exists or he does not.

Being a Grandma

Sitting at my kitchen table, I munch
a peanut-butter cookie and recall
how you did this with me, Grandma,
a memory I'd forgotten till now,

and I smile at Allison, the grandgirl
I never imagined in my childhood dreams
about my future life and family, unable
or unwilling to see myself a gray-haired

grandmother. I never imagined her,
blonde hair grown past her waist
because I read her *Grimms' Fairy Tales*
and she decided she wants to be

Rapunzel when she grows up, never
imagined sharing secrets with her,
like how, at preschool yesterday,
Jeremiah pushed her down and kissed her

because, he said, he likes her hair, it's pretty—
and I hear your throaty chuckled *That scamp!*
the day I told you how, at school, Mark kissed me
because, he said, he liked my braids, the braids

you'd woven my blonde hair into so I'd look
like Laura Ingalls—because of you,
I give Allison a squeeze, a cookie,
and a promise I won't tell anyone

if she promises not to kiss any more boys
until after she graduates college.

Grandma's Goodie Bags

Whenever we would leave your house,
you'd give us each a goodie bag,
those wrinkled paper lunch sacks stuffed
with what we nicknamed "Jessie bars"—

a chocolate-chip pan cookie pried
hot from the pan and dropped too soon
into a twist-tie sandwich bag,
where condensation phased the bar
from a cookie to a doughy state.

You'd balance out these rich, warm treats
with apples, raisins, peanuts, plums,
or overripe bananas, sure
they'd counteract the damage done
our diets by the cookie bars,

then stick a folded paper towel
on top, a gentle nudge to stress
the godliness of cleanliness—
and to wipe away the evidence
you'd slipped a piece of homemade fudge

into our palms before you kissed
our heads and stood at your front door
to wave us off with your *Toodle-loo!*

Grandpa's Grief
St. Paul, Minnesota

He sits in his recliner, stares unblinking
down the hall, and says, *Well, yes, I know*
you didn't mean to leave me all alone.
You look so lovely, standing there, dear girl. . . .

And in unison we turn to see just who
he could be talking to, these words the first
he's uttered since you died, though at the church
he cried, vague, silent tears that scored the lines

beneath his eyes. He hasn't slept much since—
he won't get in the bed you shared. We've tried
to make him eat, but he refuses, sighs,
and turns his head away, lips pinched—he's lost,

confused, senility and Alzheimer's
too much for him to more than sense, we thought,
your death. But now he smiles and in a soft,
clear voice says once again, *So lovely, dear.*

We do not ask. We know he speaks to you.
We wonder what he sees, why you've appeared,
what you are saying. . . . His tone, so warm, sincere,
is one we've never heard him use before

with you. When silence stretches, showing us
your conversation's ended, we breathe a coarse,
collective sigh. He reaches for his worn
leather Bible case, removes a cache

of photographs, and hands them to the chaplain.
She looks through all the pictures, gently asks,
Oh, who is this young lady? and he laughs,
I met her roller skating. Yes. She was

my girl, my life. She passed away in March
and rests now at Fort Snelling. I went there once
to see her, but. . . . He clears his throat and shrugs.
I know she doesn't like to be alone,

but I won't be going back till I can stay.
She understands. She told me she will wait.
That's why she came to visit me today.

Two Small Amethysts

I never thought to ask you why you loved them. When you died, I looked at you before the funeral director closed the coffin's lid, and I was stunned by how thin your hands had become. I know your hands well, the square palms, short fingers, rounded fingertips. They are my mother's hands, and mine, my daughter's hands, and now my granddaughter's. I remembered your hands holding pieces of amethyst as you showed me how the translucent purples flashed red and let me run my finger along their raw, triangular edges while you murmured, *Aren't they soothing?* above my head.

I never thought to love them like you did. To me, they were just another item you collected, like the teacups painted with sprays of purple irises and the tapestry maps of Australia suspended from your living room walls. I liked them because their marbled violet glossiness reflected the sunlight that shone through your picture window.

I never thought to ask you what they gave you. Did they give you the acceptance you were denied? Did they give you the courage to face those days after Grandpa said, *There isn't any such thing as a nervous breakdown. You need to pray through and renew your faith in God*, and walked away from you instead of praying with you? Did they give you the love that he, and later the rest of us, ladled out to you only when we could spare the time? Did they give you peace when senility finally freed you to speak your mind after forty-nine years of silence?

I never thought I'd have them sitting on my desk. But I bought two small amethysts, one for me and one for you.

farmwife elegy

air musty
        with the dust
                of forgotten potpourri
she hand- and home-made

from sweet iris roots
        and tea-cup roses she grew
                beside her
back porch steps

their scent wind-
        wafting through
                her wooden screen door, always
open, welcoming,

now drifting across
        the porch to where her empty
                rocker sways
rhythm to

gospel songs,
        lace sachets,
                farmhouse family memories
she hand- and home-made

My Grandmother's Last Letter
After Hart Crane

The irises no longer bloom
except in memory.
Yet how much room for memory there is
in the graceful scent of March winds.

There is even room enough
for the last letter my mother's mother,
Jessie,
wrote and hid between Psalms
in her mother's family Bible,
blurred almost illegible,
a spider's web in fall.

Over the silence of such space
words must be waltzed.
They are hanging echoes in visible white breaths.
They undulate like purple-blossomed stems.

And I ask myself:

"Are your fingers bold enough to pluck
old strings that are but shadows:
Is your refrain soft enough
to harmonize with its source
and it with you in chords
she would have played?"

If my grandmother could lead me by the hand
through what she could not vocalize,
I would not falter. But the winds continue luring me
with such an odor of illusions, faintly sweet.

Footprints of the Ancestors

The gaze of your accent on my memories,
the rustle of your writing on old photographs,
the cadence of your letter as you stood
on the precipice of being as forgotten in death
as you were in life—

In the Dreaming, you travel the tracks
of our ancestral past and place:
you walk with our Creator Spirit Being,
sing the sacred of our homeland
and our maternal lore—

As the rainbow connects heaven to earth,
as prayer connects humanity to God,
as grace connects God to humanity,
as blood connects me to you
and spirit you to me—

So I plant irises in my garden,
so I embrace this empty page,
so I walk the rhythms of your songs
and petition God for words both He and you
would have me sing.

Green's View Road

A narrow, two-lane avenue unwinds
In gentle curve amid the stark white oak
And slender needles of the shortleaf pines
To drift away beneath a fine-spun cloak
Of snow that blurs the sharpened edges etched
When autumn's colors blazed the branches bare.
One oak, its trunk and limbs discreetly sketched
In filigrees of ice, does not despair;

With arms outstretched, it patiently awaits
The *sotto voce* psalm of spring's return
And tries in solemn tones to resonate
The promise of rebirth it can discern—
The whispered confidences of this day,
The secrets of the shadows tinted gray.

Endnotes

1 Quoted from The Oxford Book of War Poetry

Line 1: "War in Heaven," John Allan Wyeth, Jr;
line 2: "Ode to the Confederate Dead," Allen Tate;
line 3: "Two Voices," Edmund Blunden;
line 4: "Elegy for a Dead Soldier," Karl Shapiro;
line 5: "The Spanish Descent," Daniel Defoe;
line 6: "Sonnets from China," W. H. Auden;
line 9: "Childe Harold's Pilgrimage," George Gordon Noel, Lord Byron;
line 10: "The Send-Off," Wilfred Owen;
line 11: "The Foreign Gate," Sidney Keyes;
line 12: "Sohrab and Rustum," Matthew Arnold.

Line one taken from Twentieth-Century American Poetry, edited by Dana Gioia, David Mason, and Meg Schoerke; all other lines taken from The Oxford Book of War Poetry, edited by Jon Stallworthy.

2 Lines taken from The Norton Anthology of Poetry, 5th Ed: John Pope's "Caedmon's Hymn"; Seamus Heaney's "Beowulf"; Richard Hamer's "Riddles 1 and 2," "The Wife's Lament," and "The Seafarer"; and Ezra Pound's "The Seafarer."

3 All lines taken from the New American Standard Bible, as follows:

       lines 1, 7, 13—Deuteronomy 11:18;
       lines 2, 8, 14—Song of Solomon 1:15;
       line 3—Song of Solomon 6:10;
       line 4—Isaiah 49:16;
       line 5—Isaiah 43:1;
       line 6—Psalm 68:13;
       line 9—Jeremiah 31:3;
       line 10—Proverbs 3:5;
       line 11—Psalm 37:3;
       line 12—Matthew 11:28.

4 After the cover art for A.E. Stallings' Olives: Poems, copyright The Trustees of the British Museum / Art Resource, N.Y.